"BREAKING

FREE"

By

Prophetess Rosie Mullen

"Ye shall know the truth and the truth shall make you free".

John 8:32

"BREAKING FREE"

ISBN: 978-0-578-17301-6

Published by: G & R Publishing

Publishingg.r@gmail.com

Grpublishingco.com

TABLE OF CONTENTS

Acknowledgements

This book is dedicated to my wonderful husband, Gregory Mullen. Your support has exemplified the true manifestations of love created by God to be shared between a husband and wife. Thank you greatly for allowing the Spirit of the Lord to continue to speak into your spirit. I also would like to thank my five beautiful children LaSondra, Genesis, Trinity, Miracle, and Gregory Jr. The Word of God says, "Honor thy father and thy mother….." Your love and support has exemplified the epitome of true love. I would not dare to continue without acknowledging Brenda Lovelady-Spahn who has been a great inspiration to me. To my covenant partner and friend, Minister Betty Jackson, I thank you for your prolonging desire to fast and pray with me. I will never forget you. Bishop Earnest L. Palmer, I want you to know that I think you are the best Pastor on this side of Heaven. Thanks for all you have done for me and my family. Last and most importantly I would like to

4

dedicate this book to God's hurting children. My prayer is that this book will encourage your spirit. My desire is to reinforce what God has already said, "I came so that you may have life, and have it more abundantly". In order to feel that inherited life you must become acquainted with your time of "Breaking Free". God has given us the power to speak against our hurts. If you are homeless, battered, feeling hopeless, have been molested, or abused, don't worry. After reading this book you will realize that your help (Jesus) is already with you. God bless you all for your inspiration. I love you all!

Rosie Mullen

LISTEN TO THE WIND

In times of loneliness

When you need a friend

Don't worry yourself

Just listen to the wind

When there are demons and devils

You think you can't defend

Don't be afraid

Just listen to the wind

If there is a religious ceremony

That you want to

But can't attend

Don't be too upset

Just listen to the wind

While listening

It is God talking

Eternal life

He wants to extend

So if you want to be set free

Just listen to the wind

LaSondra Mullen Copyright © 2007

NATURE'S TOUCH

I feel nature's soft touch

Like a mother's love

She sound like a singing angel

One from above

She's there to hug you

Whenever you are sad

She picks you up

When you have fallen

Kisses and makes you glad

Can't you feel the love for her?

Touching your dear heart

It's like a child and his or her mother

Whom you can never break apart

Nature's flowers that I touch

Are beautiful as they bloom

That's why in my heart for nature

There is always plenty of room

PREFACE

"The Spirit of the Lord is upon me because He has anointed me to preach the Gospel to the poor. He has sent me to heal the broken hearted, to preach deliverance to the captives and recovery of sight to the blind, to set at liberty them that are bruised.

Luke 4:18

Due to my background, training, experience, and counseling, I have come to the conclusion that hurting people are in need of more consideration. It is my goal to instruct and inspire, as well as offer assistance to those who are attempting to break free.

This book will provide certain strengths to help those who are hurting and bound. I was sitting and meditating on His Word and God began to speak to me. God showed me the pain of being in chains of addiction, abuse, discouragement, depression, hurt, and those things that has stagnated our growth.

This book will provide uplifting and inspiring words that will encourage you. It will give you direction from the Word of God through His scriptures and various experiences that I have seen happen in ministering at the shelters and out on the streets.

I believe that once a person recognizes that there are chains holding them, they are much closer to "breaking free".

This book may not cover everything, but it is based on the Word of God, my life experiences, and sermons that have played a significant part of my recovery. My prayer is that this book will be of assistance to you in becoming more familiar recognizing with understanding your problems, hurts, and pains, so that you can overcome and break free to reach your destiny.

I send this book on a mission in the mighty name of Jesus!

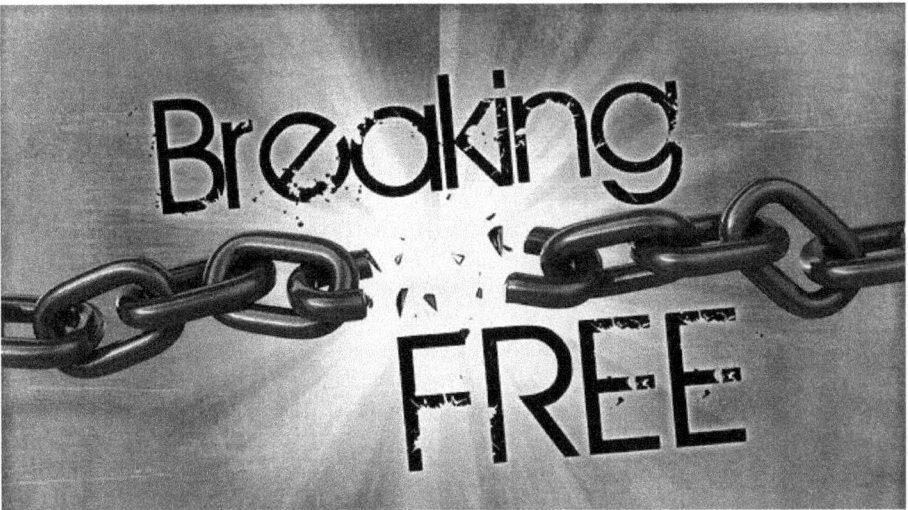

ABOUT THE AUTHOR

Rosie Mullen was born July 4th 1966, in Gainesville, AL, the fourth child of P. S. and Christine Jenkins. She is a 1984 graduate of Livingston High School in Livingston, AL. She was married to Gregory K. Mullen in July of 1985 and they have five children. Rosie grew up knowing that something was different about her but just could not pinpoint what it was until in 1997 when she heard the Voice of God tell her she had been chosen for a special purpose. She was licensed to preach by Bishop Earnest L. Palmer at the Cornerstone Full Gospel Baptist Church in 1998 and Ordained by Pastor Gregory K. Mullen and The Fairview Baptist Church in 2002.

Rosie is a giver, a lover of life and family, a wife, a mother and a prophetic woman of God. God has given her a strong compassion for hurting women, to the point that she can feel their pain. She did volunteer work with Jessie's Place and The Lovelady Center, both of which are homes for women and children.

Rosie is a graduate of Miles College with a B. S. Degree in Business Administration. She received her MBA in Accounting and Human Resources from Argosy University. She spent fifteen years in secular employment but has now taken the leap of faith to become the Chief Financial Officer with a Transitional Facility. She has done theological studies at Birmingham Baptist Bible College.

"BREAKING

FREE"

Chapter One

SALVATION

…..Verily, verily I say unto thee, except a man be born again, he cannot see the kingdom of God.

John 3:3

God's gift of salvation is the most precious gift man can or will ever receive. The power of this gift is far greater that the thoughts of men. Nothing can compare to God's merciful, and love coated, grace. God's greatest desire is to repair the souls of lost sinners and to return them to His everlasting fellowship.

God seeks those who are hopeless. He especially designed His salvation plan for those who are lost, and those who have resisted His great plan; and are now facing judgment and headed toward eternal damnation. The peace in God's salvation is one of those things that can only be understood by enduring trials and tribulations. Sometimes it takes a spiritual workout to obtain spiritual muscles.

> *"But when the right time came, the time God decided on, he sent his Son, born of a woman, born as a Jew, to buy freedom for us who were slaves to the law so that he could adopt us as his very own sons. And because we are his sons, god has sent the Spirit of his Son into our hearts, so now we can rightly speak of God as our dear Father. Now we are no longer slaves but God's own sons, everything he has belongs to us, for that is the way God planned."*
>
> *Galatians 4:4-7*

The Bible uses several words to describe salvation. In classical Greek, the verb *sozo* (to save), and the noun *soteria* (salvation), are used for the concept of rescue, deliverance, and wellness. It means to heal, preserve, and to make whole. A saved person has the authority over the enemy and has the ability to easily escape harm's way. *Sozo* and *Soteria* were mentioned intentionally and incredibly designed so that we can be delivered from the torture of the enemy and the sin he entices us to fall into. God doesn't find joy in punishing us when we sin. He would much rather eradicate us from suffering punishment and offer a life of holiness through His great love.

In the Four Gospels, salvation is clearly connected to the Old Testament because it is the manifestation of what had been prophesied about the coming of Christ. Why is this so? The Old Testament was a time of living by the law. However, the New Testament lets us know that Jesus came to fulfill the law. The Old Testament lets us know that the Messiah is coming one day. In the New Testament He was born, died, resurrected, and offered us salvation and eternal life with Him.

There are many biblical terms to recognize true salvation. Some of the most common terms used by man are, atonement, conversion, justification, reconciliation, redemption, salvation, and save.

"Atonement" is derived from the Hebrew language and means, "to cover or cancel", the covering of sin. The Bible reminds us of God's grace, mercy, and love towards us. He forgives us when we repent and in turn, throws our sins into the sea of forgetfulness, never addressing our faults again.

The question was asked, "Does that mean I can be a sinner and still have salvation?" No, that is not what this means. It means to make a conscious decision to do what is pleasing to God and not to take advantage of God's system. Consequently, if you do fall short into sin, know that true repentance is received, and accepted by God. When God forgives us, our sins are completely forgotten by Him.

The term "conversion" is described in the Webster's dictionary as, "an experience associated with the definite and decisive adoption of a religion" or "to turn around". This is the time when a conscious decision is made and understood;

A time when one totally surrenders his/her life to the Lord Jesus Christ, confesses, and recognizes that they cannot live this life to its fullness without the help of the Lord. One must have a **made-up** mind during this time of conversion in order for the conversion to be true and definite.

> *Jesus called a small child over to him and set the little fellow down among them, and said, "Unless you turn to God from your sins and become as a little children, you will never get into the Kingdom of Heaven. Therefore anyone who humbles himself as this little child is the greatest in the*

Kingdom of Heaven. And any of you who welcomes a little
child like this because you are mine is welcoming me and
caring for me."

Matthew 18:2-5

"Justification" is often used to describe being, "officially authorized" and used as the determining factor of the worthiness of mankind to God's salvation. There is a difference in justification as it pertains to a sinner versus a sinner saved by grace. Even though, "We all have sinned and come short of the glory of God" there is a great difference when we are being judged by God. If a sinner is faced with judgment and has no alibi or someone to defend him, he is damned for the death penalty. Remember God forgives us and disregards the sin as if it never existed. It is more beneficial to sin with God in your life than to sin without Him. Without God the non-repenting sinner does not stand a chance.

> *Since all have sinned and come short of the glory of God;*
> *they are now justified by his grace as a gift, through the*
> *redemption that is in Christ Jesus, whom God put forward*
> *as a sacrifice of atonement by his blood, effective through*
> *faith. He did this to show his righteousness, because in his*
> *divine forbearance he had passed over the sins previously*
> *committed….."*

Romans 3:23-25

"Reconciliation" is another term used when referring to salvation and it legally walks hand in hand with justification. It means, "To restore friendship, harmony, or to settle differences". I am reminded of the time when Adam and Eve sinned against God by eating the fruit of "The Tree of Knowledge of Good and Evil". Adam and Eve dined from the tree and immediately they both recognized their nakedness. They suffered a spiritual separation from God, which resulted in a Spiritual death. Even though God punished them for their sins, His original desire for man to live in fellowship with Him was not discarded. This is the very reason why God create the plan to send His son, Jesus, to die and be resurrected. He wanted to redeem His original plan of fellowship. The punishment in which God allocates to you has everything to do with His love for you.

God's salvation reconciles our relationship with Him even after we have been separated from Him due to our sinful behavior.

"Redemption" is another word related to salvation and originated from the Greek language. This word means, "to cut away, to sever, or to deliver". Through redemption we are victorious in overcoming the power of difficult and habitual sins. Only God has the power to rescue us from sin. It is His redemptive supremacy that allows us the strength not to relapse back in to the sin again.

God + His Redemption = Delivering Power

God's redemption brings delivering power. I am sure you have heard the saying, "The places I used to go, I don't go anymore,

18

and the friends I used to have, I don't have them anymore." It is very difficult to separate ourselves from the memories of our past. Only by relying on God and His redemptive power can we triumph over our stumbling blocks victoriously. God doesn't allow us to be saved **in** our sins, but to be saved **from** our sins. Redemption is used in the Bible to inform us that God's salvation has the power to not only save us from the consequences and punishments of sin; but also to deliver us from its power by severing (cutting away) sin from our inner character.

> *".....who gave himself for us that he might redeem us from all iniquity and purify for himself a people of his own who are zealous for good deeds?"*

> *Titus 2:14*

19

Let's take some time out and imagine the exhaustion and pain that a mother experiences as she prepares her mind to give birth to a newborn child. The mother knows ahead of time, the birth pains she will endure, yet God allows her to have the strength to not live in the present pain that she is enduring. Therefore, when it is time to give birth at another time in her life, the mother is willing.

Just as mother' are willing to repeat the process, the same goes for experiencing a spiritual "regeneration". When we are regenerated in the Spirit we are experiencing a "new birth" or "being born again". God's salvation is a Spiritual conversion that takes place in the heart, mind, and soul of a sinner who has repented. It is a time when a Spiritual metamorphosis takes place, assisted by the

Holy Spirit of God, and crosses a threshold in our life; converting our attitude, character, and devotion to a righteous life in God.

"He saved us, not because of any works of righteousness that we had done, but according to his mercy, through the water of rebirth and renewal by the Holy Spirit. This Spirit he poured out on us richly through Jesus Christ our Savior, so that, having been justified by his grace, we might become heirs according to the hope of eternal life.

Titus 3:5-7

Jesus replied, "With all the earnest I possess I tell you this: Unless you are born again, you can never get into the Kingdom of God. "Born again!" exclaimed Nicodemus. "What do you mean? How can an old man go back into his mother's womb and be born again?" Jesus replied, "What I am telling you so earnestly is this: Unless one is born of water and the Spirit, he cannot enter the Kingdom of God. Men can only reproduce human life, but the Holy Spirit gives new life from heaven; so don't be surprised at my statement that you must be born again! Just as you can hear the wind but can't tell where it comes from or where it will go next, so it is with the Spirit. We do not know on whom he will next bestow his life from heaven." "What do you mean?" Nicodemus asked. Jesus replied, "You, a respected Jewish teacher, and yet you don't understand these things? I am telling you what I know and have seen---and yet you won't believe me. But if you don't even believe me when I tell you about such things as these that happen here among men, how can you possibly believe if I tell you what is going on in heaven? For only I, the Messiah, have come to earthy and will return to heaven again. And as Moses in the wilderness lifted up the bronze image of a serpent on a pole, even so I must be lifted up on a pole, so that anyone who believes in me will have eternal life.

John 3:3-15

Being "saved" is to be taken under God's great wings of love and delivered from the influences of sin, set free, and made whole. "She will bear a son, and you are to name him Jesus, for he will save his people from their sins."

Matthew 1:21

(Words of Jesus) "If anyone hears me and doesn't obey me, I am not his judge—for I have come to save the world and not to judge it. But all who reject me and my message will *be judged at the Day of Judgment by the truths I have spoken."*

John 12:47-48

"How true it is, and how I long that everyone should know it, that Christ Jesus came into the world to save sinners."

I Timothy 1:15

"For God so loved the world that he gave his only Son, so that everyone who believes in him may not perish but may have eternal life. Indeed, God did not send the Son into the world to condemn the world, but in order that the world might be saved through him. Those who believe in him are not condemned; but those who do not believe are condemned already, because they have not believed in the name of the only Son of God. And this is the judgment, that the light has

come into the world, and people loved darkness rather than light because their deeds were evil. For all who do evil hate the light and do not come to the light, so that their deeds may not be exposed. But those who do what is true come to the light, so that it may be clearly seen that their deeds have been done in God."

John 3:16-21

"Then everyone who calls on the name of the lord shall be saved."

Acts 2:21

"Because of his kindness, you have been saved through trusting Christ. And even trusting is not of yourselves; it too is a gift from God. Salvation is not a reward for the good we have done, so none of us can take any credit for it. It is God himself who has made us what we are and given us new lives from Christ Jesus; and long ages ago he planned that we should spend these lives in helping others."

Ephesians 2:8-10

"Then he saved us---not because we were good enough to be saved but because of his kindness and pity---by washing away our sins and giving us the new joy of the indwelling Holy Spirit, whom he poured out upon us with wonderful fullness---and all because of what Jesus Christ our Savior did so that he could declare us good in God's eyes---all because of his great kindness; and now we can share in the wealth of the eternal life he gives us, and we are eagerly looking forward to receiving it. These things I have told you are all true. Insist on them so that Christians will be careful to do good deeds all the time, for this is not only right, but it brings results."

Titus 3:5

Then finally, "salvation", Is the umbrella that oversees justification, reconciliation, and redemption. God's salvation saves, redeems, justifies, regenerates, converts, reconciles, and atones.

This Jesus is 'the stone that was rejected by you, the builders; it has become the cornerstone.' There is salvation in no one else, for there is no other name under heaven given among mortals by which we must be saved."

Acts 4:11-12

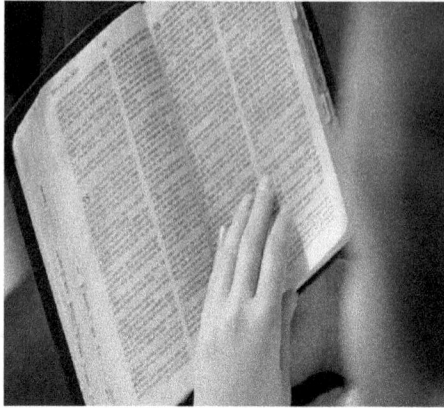

The New Testament teaches that Jesus Christ is the source of salvation. When we think of source, we think of the root, beginning, or the original foundation of where things begin.

The New Testament teaches us about Jesus Christ being the source of our salvation. Jesus is like the foundation on which a home is built upon. If the foundation is not set correctly, the entire house will fall. Without Jesus in your life, you have no foundation. It is now time to stand strong, because a man in a crumbling state is too weak to reach his breakthrough.

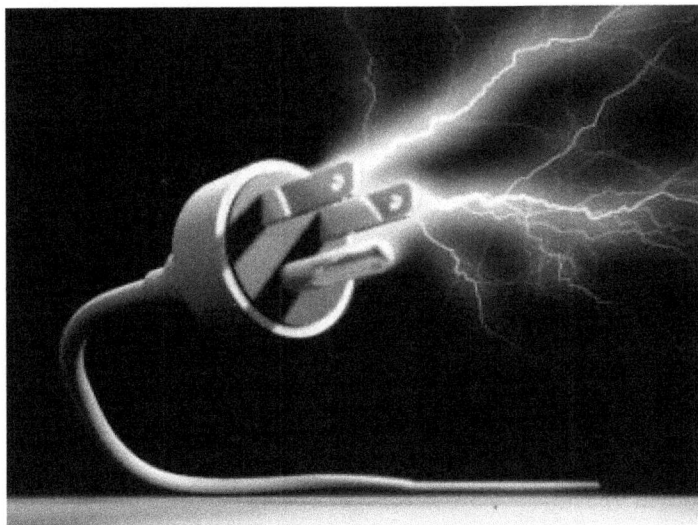

Electricity is a natural phenomenon and existed way before scientists discovered it and how it operated. The ancient Greek and Parthian civilizations learned of static electricity by rubbing objects against fur. The Parthians may also have had some knowledge of electroplating, based on the discovery of the Baghdad Battery, which resembles a Galvanic cell. Benjamin Franklin conducted extensive research in electricity. His theories on the relationship between lightning and static electricity, including his famous kite-flying experiment, sparked the interest of later scientists whose work provided the basis for modern electrical technology. Notably these include Luigi Galvani (1737-1798), Alessandro Volta (1745-1827), Michael Faraday (1791-1867), Andre'-Marie Ampere (1775-1836), and George Simon Ohm (1789-1854). The late 19th and early 290th century produced such giants of electrical engineering such as Nikola Tesla, Samuel Morse, Antonio Meucci, Thomas Edison, George

Westinghouse, Werner von Siemens, Charles Steinmetz, and Alexander Graham Bell. Even after all of the noble discoveries of these great men, the truth is that none of the lights that they experimented with turned on without its main source of power.

This same analogy coincides with Jesus, once we connect to the chief source (Jesus), we receive power to operate. Jesus is the nucleus of our salvation, Jesus must be the most important part of our being in order to be delivered and set free. Jesus is the only one who can break the chains of addiction. You may be suffering from the addiction of pornography, drugs, money, self, love, fear, past hurts, depression, cigarettes, tattoos, body piercing, gang involvement, stealing, adultery, or fornication. It doesn't matter what demon the enemy has sent your way. The Father, gives us the strength to walk away the only way to connect to this powerful source is by connecting to JESUS CHRIST.

> *Therefore I endure all things for the elect's sakes that they may also obtain the salvation which is in Christ Jesus with eternal glory.*
>
> *2 Timothy 2:10*

God allowed Jesus, His only son, to pay for our sins by visiting death. We deserve to be placed on death row because of our sins, but God's love for us has released us. Salvation gives us that light source we need in order to be led towards freedom and out of the bondages of life. The Bible says:

"Whom the Son sets free is free indeed".

John 8:36

To be bound by drugs or abuse causes tremendous sorrow in the lives of many. With the Lord Jesus Christ as the head of your life, you too, can "break free". The first step to becoming free is to allow God to be the spark of your Spirit. In order to experience real freedom you must search, find, and love God.

Search, Find, and Love God

Are you one of those who are bound by sin? Do you want to get out of your situation, escape the life you have been living, and turn to God? You may not know where to begin. I want to assure you that with Jesus as the head of your life, YOU CAN "Break Free". Command the enemy to loose you in the name of Jesus. Let him know that you will no longer be bound and shackled by him and his mischievous spirit. Demand your joy back! Stand up, and trust God, then watch and see how He will begin to work in your life.

I've done that, now what?

Be willing to sacrifice yourself. Give yourself to God for the sake of salvation. How determined and motivated are you to get the freedom that you deserve? Accept Jesus Christ as your Lord and Savior. This is your next step.

Jesus told Nicodemus:

Marvel not that I said unto thee, ye must be born again.

John 3:7

Blessed are those who hunger and thirst for righteousness, for they will be filled.

Matthew 5:6

Being bound deprives us from fulfilling our destiny.

When we become preoccupied with our burdens, we lose sight of the direction in which God desires for us to go. Living in bondage promotes depression and eventually takes ma toll on our spirit.

When we are spiritually bound, we are living in death. You can be spiritually free if you allow the Spirit of God to light the candle to your spirit. God will then begin to speak His Spirit into yours, causing an ultimate release. How far are you willing to go? How bad do you want to be free? Come to the place where you thirst for your deserved freedom. If you have a hunger for freedom, then you will be willing to do whatever it takes to attain it.

God ended bondage when He sent Jesus to die for our sins, and constructed the Canon (Bible) for us to digest, to obey, and comply with. The Bible is recognized many times throughout the Word of God as a sword. This sword is a weapon of protection and every Word in the Bible is one of the ways in which God communicates with us. God desires for us to embed this Sword (The Word of God) into our spirits. Through obeying God's Word, we shall be delivered from bondage and receive salvation. Always remember, those things that are not of God, will ambush us and anything that is of God, sets us free.

You must be born again and make the choice to repent and allow God to be the God He promised us He'd be. God will bless you if you allow Him to have control of your life. Will you accept Him today?

Chapter Two

ADMITTING, CONFESSING & PRAYING

Confess your faults one to another, and pray one for another that you may be healed…..

James 5:16

A very important key to "breaking free" is to first *admit* you have a problem. Living in denial hinders you from being released. You must admit to yourself and confess to the Lord, "I have a problem. My problem is _____ and I need you Lord, to help me "break free" so that I can now reside in your will". As long as you live in a state of denial, you will always be bound by whatever is haunting you. It doesn't matter whether its drugs or alcohol, molestation, or rape, the strain of bondage will continue to control your life.

> *"Hello, my name is Lisa and I was an alcoholic. I am overjoyed at being here today and can honestly admit that I am clean and sober. By the grace of God, and His unconditional love for me, as of December, this year I will have 19 m years free and sober.*
>
> *As each year arises, I look forward to the Christmas holidays. I become overwhelmed with fear of the unknowing.*

It was this same month, nineteen years ago when I first began my unbreakable journey in bondage. This is the time when the devil sent one of his recruits my way to offer me one small dink. That one small drink took over the next nineteen years of my life. I was twenty years old when I began. I was already saved, sanctified, and baptized with the Holy Ghost. I knew what it meant to praise, worship and to have a strong hunger for God's Word. I had even begun to speak in tongues.

However, on this particular day, the devil was able to imprison me. He came on a day when my guards were down. Never did I know that one small drink on that day would have had the impact on my life that it did. On that day I became a slave placed in bondage to alcohol. Alcohol became my god. I thought about it when I awoke in the morning and when I lay my head down to sleep at night. Many times, during the day,

the thought of it saturated my thinking pattern. Eventually, I became malfunctioned. I was unable to continue working my job of four years. My life came to a screeching halt. My family and friends constantly insisted that I enroll into an alcohol rehabilitation program. But my addiction had me so enslaved, that I refused to entertain the thought of it.

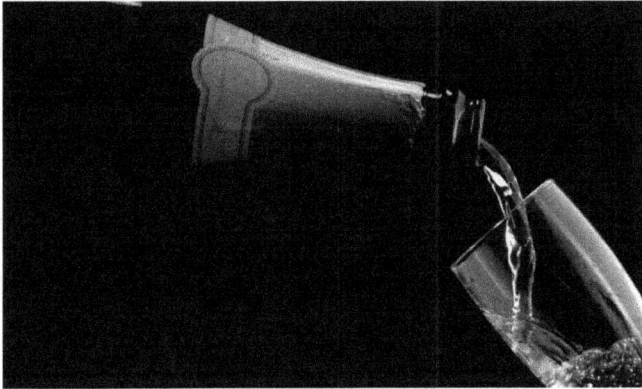

Finally after nineteen years, while sitting in a local park, next to a small church on Picket Street, I sat listening to the songs from the local church choir. The angelic voices that rang from the small church seemed to overtake the airwaves that day. They were singing "No weapon formed against me shall prosper". I remember complaining to Jesus as the song continued to be sang saying, "If no weapon formed against me shall prosper, why am I here and not inside that church?"

Then the Spirit of the Lord spoke to my spirit and said, "If I wanted to be inside that church, I needed to get up on my own two feet and walk inside".

I remember arguing with myself that morning. One side of me said to, "Shut up and keep drinking". The same voice repeatedly reminded me that I was worthless, dirty, and a lost case. The other voice kept repeating, softly and with sincerity saying, "I will never leave you nor forsake you".

It was in that moment that I recognized, admitted, and confessed to the Lord, "I have a problem". Before I knew it, I was standing inside that church kneeling at the altar, repenting and pleading to god saying, "Please save me".

The Pastor asked me if there was a particular need that I was in prayed for. I looked him directly in his eyes and said, "I am admitting to God that I am a sinner, bound by alcohol. Now I realize that He is the only One who can completely deliver me. My prayer is that God will forgive me for all of my wrong doings, save me, and teach me to be the woman of God He designed for me to be. I want to break free".

An anonymous yet common testimony

A person who pronounces, "I can quit whenever I want to" is generally a person who feels as though they alone are tough enough to stand up against the powers of Satan. Jesus is the only one who possesses that type of authority. God wants us to depend on Him to fight and conquer our battles. However, there are some requirements:

Requirement #1 – admit and come to grips with the truth; you have a problem!

NOTE: Failing to admit causes weakness and instability. You must admit who you are, what you are, and what you have been through to God in order for the healing process to begin. Face the facts! If you refuse, the problem is compressed and pushed back into your bosom where it has been most comfortable all along, placing you in a doomed place of no escape.

Requirement #2 – Acknowledge the need for God's assistance.

Too many people today are living in a covered up world. Many hours are being wasted on hiding behind and suppressing problems. Suppressing problems is not acceptable by God. We must bring the hurt and pain to the surface and deal with it in order to break free from all of the things that bind us.

It's time to walk away from your past and into your destiny. The past is exactly what it means. The past is yesterday's problem. In 1 Peter 5:8, it warns us about our adversary (the devil) who "prowls about like a roaring lion, seeking to devour." The Bible calls him, "The tempter, the seducer, and the accuser." Satan will do everything in his power to overpower his prey (you), Satan will go as far as to dig up your past troubles and use them against you to destroy you. With Jesus Christ on the front line in battle for you, Satan is hopeless in his attempt to destroy your life. The Lord has made it exceptionally easy for us to overcome our state of bondage. He has instructed for us to confess our faults, pray, believe, and depend on Him, and wait to receive our break through.

Confess your faults one to another, and pray one for another that you may be healed.

James 5:16

To whom should we confess? God desires for us to confess our sins to Him. I'm reminded of the story in Exodus, when the Israelites defeated the Amalek army. This was a result of Moses holding his staff in the air and remaining constantly in prayer throughout the battle. Whenever Moses held up his hand, Israel prevailed; and whenever he lowered his hand in fatigue the Amaleks prevailed. The momentum of the battle continued to fluctuate repeatedly until Aaron and Hur came alongside Moses to assist him in holding up his tired arms. Aaron and Hur both propped Moses up on a rock, then the Israelites were victorious throughout the remainder of the battle.

You are also equipped with this kind of battle-winning and breaking free ability. Through consistent prayer, you will draw upon the five basic lessons that are contained within Moses' story. Even though we'd like to think we are self-sufficient and self-reliant individuals, the reality is that we must totally rely on the strength of

God. Moses arms eventually became weak and unable to hold up his staff. He depended on God to send him what he needed to endure. Can you imagine the amount of conversation (prayer) Moses, Aaron, and Hur were engulfed in as they waited on God? They spent hours in praying and asking God to strengthen them so that they could win the war. Take time out of your day, and pray not only for yourself, but also for your brothers and sisters in the Lord. Dedicate yourself to long conversations with Him about your situations.

We need to develop creative ways of reminding ourselves of who created us and how special we are to God. Know without a doubt who you are praying to when you pray. You should be praying for those in your community, at school, on your job, and even at social events.

Don't hesitate to come seek covenant prayer partner who are willing to join you in prayer. Go to the ministers, pastors, and saints; reveal to them how the enemy has had you under attack. Allow them to stand in intercessory prayer for you. There are two changes that will take place. One, the devil will get mad, and two, the Lord will bless you over and above your circumstances.

Imagine driving your car on a hot summer day and suddenly it begins wobbling. That's when the human instinct protrudes through your lips, "Oh my God, I have a flat tire. Lord help me." Now you are stranded on the side of the road. You have no tools and you have no knowledge on how to repair a flattened tire. Finally, someone stops to lend you a hand. Would you tell them what the problem is or would you just have them wander around trying to figure out what you need?

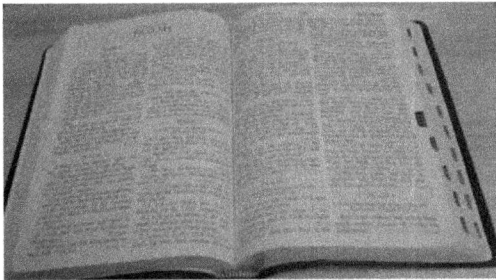

You would most likely inform them that you have a problem and tell them what the problem is, so that they can better assist you.

By informing your aide about your flat tire, you have admitted to them that you have a problem. Also, keep this in mind. God is always listening when we call on him during those first few stressful seconds of a dilemma. He hears you confessions and is there to assist you!

Learn to place yourself in a comfort zone so that you are willing to open up to others who are agreeing in prayer with you; feel free to release those things that are holding you in captive.

Note: Possessing the ability to release your downfalls through speaking is the beginning of your healing process.

Let's paraphrase for a moment. Our bodies were created to tolerate the intake of food, digest it, and then separate those nutrients that are healthy for us, and discard the poisons that are unhealthy. Likewise in our Spiritual lives, there is so much worldly junk that we take in daily. We consume past hurts and so an exuberant amount of pain. These emotional stresses of life have been deposited into our spiritual systems, and we have allowed these negative steps to overtake us. Now it is time to take back those things that are rightfully ours. The devil and his demons are not allowed to be seated comfortably in your life. Confess to God the presence of the enemy. Intake more of God and His Word and discard those things of the enemy. We have the authority and the power to separate those things. Just tell God!

Often we seek prayer from others, yet, we don't give them the meat of our prayer. We are only willing to share those things that cause us to look good in the eyesight of others. Don't be afraid to share your needs with those who care enough to pray for you. Remember, we all have sin and have fallen short of the glory and honor of God." When you learn to expose the devil, and trust God to stand in your defense, you will "break free" from all of the things that bind you.

Eat the Chicken and Discard of the Bones

There is a saying that says, "Eat the chicken and discard the bones". This metaphor describes the times when we confess our faults one to another. This is the time when the saints are praying. This is the time when the prayers of the righteous are being elevated vibrantly and great healing is taking place. This is the time when fasting and prayer are both knocking at the gates of Heaven, expecting a release for you from your place of captivity. Once you are able to talk about it, then you can begin the healing process. Our spirits are possessed with painful scares from our past. You have authority over those negative spirits. Tell them to, "Get out! In the name of Jesus! You cannot have a seat here! Don't even think about being comfortable!" After this time of confessing Jesus as Lord, the Spirit of God is so potent, that His Spirit will stay and the enemy will be discarded from your life. We must be willing to discard those things that are not good for us. This is the time when the breaking free process begins. Your "breakthrough" is on the way!

Pray for your healing. The scriptures instruct us to pray for one another that you may be healed. Healing is not only physical, or mental, but it is also spiritual. In order to get this healing there must be some admitting, confessing, and praying going on in the Spirit.

Warning!!! Some may feel that we can pray all alone and everything will be fine, however, God said, "Confess your faults one to another and pray for one another". You must be aware. We cannot just confess to anyone. We need to make sure that it is someone who is spiritual, loves Jesus Christ, and filled with the Holy Spirit. Paul writes to the church at Galatia:

> *"Brethren, if you see a man overtaken in a fault, ye which are spiritual, go to him in the spirit of meekness considering yourself lest you fall into temptation.*

> *Galatians 6:1*

More Truths on Confessing

It is very important to understand the concept of confessing mainly because it is a requirement of God. The word, "Confess" derives from the Greek word, "homologeo" meaning to "own up to something that you have done or to come to an agreement with God that you have sinned". Confessing has always been a problem to human nature. We tend to believe that if we confess, it will cause problems. What the nation has failed to realize is this. If we don't learn to confess the truth, our problems will amplify and persist to exist. In other words, the problem needs to be recognized and confronted by self, and dealt with. If not, expect an escalation to the problem.

Prove It Biblically – Story of Abram and Sarai

Now there was a famine in the land, and Abram went down to Egypt to live there for a while because the famine was severe. As he was about to enter Egypt, he said to his wife Sarai, "I know what a beautiful woman you are. When the Egyptians see you, they will say, 'This is his wife.' Then they will kill me but will let you live. Say you are my sister, so that I will be treated well for your sake and my life will be spared because of you." When Abram came to Egypt, the Egyptians saw that she was a very beautiful woman. And when Pharaoh's officials saw her, they praised her to Pharaoh, and she was taken into his palace. He treated Abram well for her sake, and Abram acquired sheep and

cattle, male and female donkeys, menservants and
maidservants, and camels. But The LORD inflicted serious
diseases on Pharaoh and his household because of Abram's
wife Sarai. So Pharaoh summoned Abram. "What have
you done to me?" he said. "Why didn't you tell me she was
your wife? Why did you say, 'She is my sister,' so that I took
her to be my wife? Now then, here is your wife. Take her
and go!" Then Pharaoh gave orders about Abram to his
men, and they sent him on his way with his wife and
everything he had.

Genesis 12:10-20

Abram, in the scriptures above, was already anguished with
troubles. The place where he was living was now afflicted with
rigorous starvation and he was focused to relocate his family in order
to endure. Before Abram entered Egypt, the scriptures pronounced
the fear Abram had for his life. Abram was not willing to confess the
truth about Sarai being his wife. Sarai was recognized as being very
beautiful, which caused pessimistic results in the life of Abram and
the choices he made. Abram was afraid that Pharaoh would kill him
so that he could have Sarai to himself. Abram allowed the spirit of
fear to interrupt his time of true confession. Instead Abram chose to
lie and asked Sarai to say that she was his sister and not his wife.
Isn't it something how the devil uses one person to drag another into
sin also? Abram had a desire to lie and convinced Sarai to lie also.

As the story continues, the scripture lets us know that God was not pleased and revealed to Pharaoh the truth. Pharaoh did agree and found Sarai to be attractive, and yes, he did want her to himself; however, he only wanted what was pleasing to God. When Pharaoh was enlightened with the truth about Sarai, he became angry with Abram. Now the problem that was once small had developed into a much larger problem, all because Abram wasn't willing to confess what was true.

The fear of being punished has ripped confession from our tongues.

As children we are taught the art of not confessing or to lie. Children are constantly learning, and temptations run rampant throughout their emergence into an adult. When a child does wrong, they know to expect a punishment that more than likely will not bring upon happiness. In spite of our parent's intentions, we cannot ignore the supposed common sense of the mind of humankind who would much rather escape punishment, rather than confess and face it head on. Imagine cookies from your parents cookie jar had come up missing. We were called in for questioning and no one would confess, because they knew they would have to face the consequences. Instead of confessing the truth, they learned to lie as an avenue to escape punishment. Children need to know that it is good to confess the truth and then maybe the punishment won't be as severe. Children should have an open door of communication set up between someone who they trust, so that they feel comfortable enough to speak the truth even if they are in the wrong.

"Train up a child in the way he should go; and when he is old, he will not depart from it"

Proverbs 22:6

God knows your situations far before they occur. In the Old Testament, people went to the priest and confessed their sins and issues. We need to know that we have a pastor or fellow church member who we too can trust enough to share our faults, and problems with.

If we say that we have no sin, we are deceiving ourselves and the truth is not in us.

If we confess our sins, He is faithful and righteous to forgive us our sins and to cleanse us from all unrighteousness.

I John 1:9

Confession offers a time of healing and forgiveness ultimately establishing a closer relationship with the Lord.

We spend far too much time tormenting ourselves about what others may think of us when we admit to our downfalls. It's time to forget about what you have been taught as a child. "Tell the truth, you get punished." It is far better to confess the truth and receive a lighter punishment than to lie and to receive the worst punishment. Because of God's grace, love, and mercy for us, we don't have to expect the worst. Even though we must endure punishment for sins, as Christians, we have to remember that our punishment is encompassed with an ultimate undertone of the only One who has proven love unconditionally. When Jesus died for our sins, he left an opened door to converse with Him about anything. Jesus desires for us to feel comfortable in confessing our faults to Him. God is an understanding God. He appreciates our willingness to confess to Him.

The fear of confessing continues to live in us. Confession is an act that should be learned as a child. If not, our desire to confess will diminish completely as we continue to grow.

When I was a child, I talked like a child; I thought like a child, I reasoned as a child. When I became a man, I put childish ways behind me.

I Corinthians 13:11

You are not a child anymore, face it!

It takes thirty days to form a habit. Parents should not wait until it's too late to attempt to control the new habit of avoiding confession. Teaching a child to admit their faults is a great part of training. Training is to condition the mind before a crisis occurs. It is preparation for future circumstances. The human instinct has conditioned man to escape any discussion that will admit faulty behavior. This forces the mind to lie to self and send self into a spiraling state of denial. This is another trick of the devil to bind your heart, mind, and spirit. This happens quite often in today's society along with the pressures and stresses of life that constantly accumulate. Many relationships are destroyed because we fail to simply admit and confess our problems and wrong doings. This type of behavior must cease in order to escape to freedom.

The Bible tells us in I Corinthians 13:11 says, "When I was a child, I talked like a child, I thought like a child, I reasoned as a child. When I became a man, I put childish ways behind me." There are many bad and good habits we all have learned as an innocent child, but what we learned then, should not be a stumbling block now. At some point in your life you simply have to, "Grow up!"

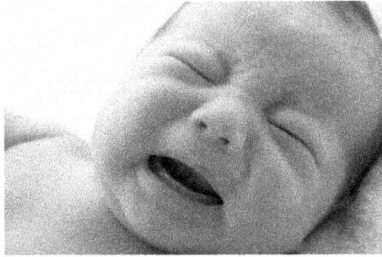

By the time we reach the age of an adult, it is a known fact, "Lies are not good". Even the sinner knows that, God wants you to repent, and confess your faults and sins to Him, then allow Him to do the rest.

When all else fails, PRAY!

Pray for your healing. Pray fervently asking God for your break through. The scripture instructs you to pray until you are healed. Jacob wrestled with God refusing to stop until he was blessed. Stay on your knees praying and fighting to take your life back. Healing is not only physical; but it is also mental and spiritual.

In order to get this healing, there must be some admitting, confessing, and praying going on in your spirit.

Some of you may feel as though you are praying alone, and you lack confidence in your ability to stand strong. If this is you, remember what the Bible says, "No weapon formed against you shall prosper". He never required for us to handle any of our trials and tribulations by ourselves.

That's God's job, don't butt it.

You've prayed, Now Release!

Many men and women miss out on the intimacies and pleasures God intended for them to have in their marriages, because they have not yet reached a point of release. Maybe you are a victim of rape or molestation. Maybe your perpetrator was a close relative, or someone whom you trusted. Maybe you have been praying, but still have not been successful in finding your release. The pressure seems to escalate daily, because you haven't conjured up enough strength to share your heart ache with anyone other than God. Many times pressure such as these destroy the intimacies of marriage. The hurts of your past have now become the hurts of today. This is because you have not given your troubles completely to the Lord. It's time for you to be purged. Peak the past out of you, and leave it at the foot of Jesus. You will be surprised at the instant break through you'll experience the moment you do. Life is bursting with regrets, frustrations, and heartbreaks. It's amazing how we tend to commit to remembering our downfalls and ignoring our accomplishments.

God has a plan for your life and He desires for you to move toward your eternal destiny. Any future given to us by God is full of promises, bursting over with delight, and jam-packed of expectations.

You have a choice to either continue to dwell in your past misfortunes or break away from your oppressed past. Boast in your faith in God and allow Him to guide you for the rest of your life. The choice is yours; God didn't create you to be sufferers to your past. Ask God for the courage to "break free" from whatever is binding you to your *past.*

......God has said, "Never will I leave you; never will I forsake you."

Hebrews 13:5

Jesus said, "He would never leave you nor forsake you". Jesus is always with you. Be willing to put your own agenda aside to follow wherever God leads you.

Forget My Past?

Does this mean we are supposed to forget about everything we have ever experienced in the past? How will we ever have a testimony if we do?

It is fine to glance back in the past and remember it as a time of breaking free, deliverance, learning, and development of your testimony. Always be reminded of where God has brought you from. Keep in mind that the enemy will constantly attempt to use your past to dictate your present and future. Don't let your past define you. That's God's job!

"The effective, fervent prayer of a righteous man availeth much"

Delivered, But What If I Relapse?

Pray and ask the Lord to help you to place your mind in His will so you will never revert back to the things of your past. If it comes a time where you can't eat or sleep because you have been focusing on your past, you have begun to worship your problem. Your problems have strangely become your false gods. Seek God with all your heart and ask Him for that peace and comfort to overcome your past.

Here's something else that you should know. Your everyday is better than your yesterday and the best of life is yet to come. Jesus is still on the throne and at work in your life.

Expect God to continue to bless you in new ways. God was there with you in your past, was there when you came out, and will continue to guide you until your end has come. Press forward and continue to live your life abundantly and with an overload of peace and joy. Trust God to bring you an encore of overload of success.

Many times the downfalls that you experience in your life causes your heart to harden. God understands and feels your pain. When you lose a soul mate, husband, wife, or close friend, understand that God has not forgotten you. His presence is always near. He feels our every emotion. God is so awesome; He is the only God with the ability to transform past pains into a time of rejoicing. Nothing occurs in our lives unless God allows it to. Satan has no power over God. He is worthless and without reason. Your past will always be there so try not to focus on running from it. Don't try to ignore or change your past, because your past is futile to your upcoming days of exultation. Instead, ask God to help you learn to trust His sovereignty in your days to come. Don't waste time and energy trying to numb a broken heart with drugs or alcohol, denying your feelings, starting a "rebound" relationship, or trying to distract yourself with positive activities. All of the above actions are lures of distractions put in place by Satan to cause your focus to become blurred.

And he said, the things which are impossible with men are possible with God.

Luke 18:27

If your heart is torn, don't worry, God is the potter. God wants to put you back together again, but you must be willing to give Him the pieces. Turn all of the things over to Him. God desires those matters that involve your children, husband, friends, and family members. God knows just what it takes to soothe the depressed, jealous, or unforgiving heart. He holds the blueprint for reconstructing your heart. HE IS GOD! Once you understand this wholeness of God, you can give the completeness of yourself over to Him and never relapse again.

For with God nothing shall be impossible.

Luke 1:37

God is always standing by and He is prepared to heal your broken heart. Talk to Jesus and let Him know that you are in need of Him. He may not come when you want Him to, but be patient and don't complain. God has not forgotten you. Sometimes the waiting period plays a vital part in His plan to gently guide you through your healing process. Even if you feel you are losing something by waiting, just know that sometimes God will allow that for a reason. This season may have been a season for learning faith or a season where God wants you to seek a Word from Him through studying.

…..faith cometh by hearing, and hearing by the word of God

Romans 10:17

Ask Him to help you to discern those things which are good for your life, and to discard of those things which will hinder you. Seasons and people will continuously come and go throughout your life, but God always stays.

I Am Afraid I'll Fall

You are not expected by God to be successful in all you do. Face it, sometimes you will just fail. This is not a time to beat yourself. Prepare yourself to face the consequences of your actions. Take control by facing your condemnations, guilt, regrets, and self-inflicted punishments. Pray, believe, and then wait on your time to receive.

Pray + Believe + Receive = Break Through

Allow God to rejuvenate your strength, hope, and your self confidence. Spend time talking to God about your failures. He doesn't have a problem teaching you what He wants you to learn from your failures. The biggest obstacle to overcome is the ability to forgive you.

Let your unhealthy past go! Don't waste time and energy trying to hold on to someone or something from the past if that person or thing doesn't have a place in your present or future. Accept reality when you can't bring back a marriage, job, child, relationship, or anything else you're trying to resurrect. Give it over to God and then walk away. Stop trying to work the problems out yourself! This battle is not yours, it's the Lord's. Don't allow yourself to drown in sorrow over things you can't do anything about. The God we trust is a giver of new beginnings and a provider of overflowing promises.

Whenever you are on the right path with the Lord, the enemy will always show his mendacious head. Always be on guard! It is important for you to understand! Satan does not have the victory over your life! God does! Don't give up! With God before you, there is no need to worry. With God first, the idea of relapsing should not enter your mind. God has a lesson for you in all of your crossings. Allow God to strengthen your character and renew your mind, then you can become the person He wants you to become. Break free!!

Your past experiences are not solitary for your own benefit, but they are intended to be of assistance to others. Your past experiences are your testimonies and are valuable tools made available by God subconsciously for you to revert back to when ministering to others. It is necessary to use what you've learned about yourself and then press forward to encourage others to do the same.

When you get to the point where you have confessed, surround yourself with spiritual people; not those who attend church following the footsteps of tradition and their ancestors. Be selective about who you allow to pray for you and come into a covenant agreement. Only allow those who have been filled with the Holy Spirit to touch and agree with you. The wrong spirit can hinder your "breakthrough". God will send those spirit filled people into your life. Stop choosing them yourself, because it is not worth the hassle.

When I was a child being raised in the church, the saints would sing a song that said, "It's me, it's me, it's me O' Lord, standing in the need of prayer". Even though I was young, I knew it was a personal statement addressed to the Lord. We all are standing in the need of prayer. Many people have closed themselves in a pity closet, and have become weary in trying. I have news for you, giving up was never a part of the plan for your life.

There was a young man that was addicted to drugs in my hometown. I remember this young man very well. My husband and I did all that we could possibly do to be of assistance to this man. His wife had left him, he was going through a terrible time, and feeling very alone. At that time he seemed appreciative for our offered help.

He accepted his call into the ministry. After doing so, his wife came back. After she returned, his attitude shifted from humble to arrogant. He shook his Bible at us and said, "I got it!" Needless to say, he reverted back to his old drug habits and he and his wife have been divorced for years now. He never faced his drug addiction head on as a problem and because he didn't, the enemy continued to hunt him down. The root of his problem was hid failure to admit to his drug addiction and confess it to the Lord. He needed God's help to stand unyielding in his breaking free phase.

The more you smother your problems with self desires and self pride, the more damaging the problem becomes. I believe that this is the reason why many ailments, nervous breakdowns, anxiety attacks, and even heart attacks arise. You were not designed by God with the ability to tolerate the spiritual pressures of the devil without God's help. It is those things that are held inside that accumulate pressure, causing you to fall deeper into danger zones.

Some cancer patients are diagnosed with skin cancer. They show visible signs of the disease and are easily treated. On the other hand, another cancer patient has internal cancer with signs that are difficult to detect. Their symptoms can go undetected for years and cause severe internal complications. This is what happens when our problems are suppressed. God knows your problems are there, but He gives you the opportunity to invite Him into your soul to help resolve your problem. You can only deal with your problems as long as they are endurable by you. Without God, at some point, you will burst. Your spirit becomes a walking time bomb, waiting to explode. I want you to understand you don't have to get to that point. You can confess it and bring it to the surface to be dealt with while you have the time.

You were created with purpose and potential. Your past doesn't determine your future, only God does. Stay with the Lord, remember your past positively, and allow God to promote you towards your freedom.

Chapter Three

Forgiveness

You must learn to forgive others, so that you can experience your break through. Without the act of forgiveness it is virtually impossible to be free. The word, forgive, means to pardon someone for something that they have done to harm or hurt you.

Peter asked Jesus the question in Matthew 18:21, "How many times should I forgive my brother in a day, seven times?" Jesus responded by saying, "Not just seven times, but seventy times seven".

In other words the number of times to forgive is infinitely unlimited. When you forgive you are releasing a debt that has stunted your growth and in doing so you, too, are being released from being imprisoned in a place of un-forgiveness.

Many times we do not realize how important it is for us to forgive, and how it frees our mind and spirit to live a life of peace.

It is not a good feeling to be around someone that you have a grudge against. Life is too short to be overwhelmed with feelings of intense animosity, resentment, or vindictiveness. Why waste your time being hard-hearted, unforgiving, and with a mean attitude, when you can be loving, kind, and full of joy. Accept the things of your past as over and done with.

Forgiving is not always an easy task, but it must take place in order to be free and to fulfill your fate. Forgiving is a hard thing to do, yet it can be accomplished. Forgiving is an action word and it takes action to obtain a positive result. Don't be afraid to visit the root of the problem. The first step in forgiving is to consider the incident and recognize the smallness in what you have been unforgiving about. It helps to journalize your feelings about the incident. This allows you the opportunity to organize your thoughts and calm your nerves, especially if you are not good with conversing. It can become very discouraging when you go to express to someone that you have forgiven them and the words refuse to come out correctly. Try writing your thoughts on a sheet of paper. The results will be more promising. Then practice what you plan to say until you feel comfortable with it. State clearly what it is you are forgiving them for and remember to always allow Jesus to speak through you in cases like these, exemplifying love and sincerity in your heart?

❖ Acknowledge your actions without making excuses and go out of your way to avoid an argument.
❖ Stay focused on keeping peace.
❖ Share your feelings about what happened and avoid blaming, exaggerating, or making sarcastic and unnecessary statements.

Some times during the conversation, sit back and listen to the other person's response without getting defensive. They may not say the things you want to hear, but they have a right to respond. It is your duty to give them great respect! A conversation takes two or more people, one listens, while the other speaks. Many times, they simply want you to understand why they did the things they did. More than likely, when the dust settles, you will realize that the whole saga was merely a complete misunderstanding in the first place.

This is now your time to respond. This is the opportune time to express understanding and the willingness to forgive. Let them know the type of relationship you now desire to have with them. After you have done all of that, love and pray for them, then move on, don't look back, and let it go!

There is a young lady who had a hard time forgiving her father, because her father neglected his responsibility as a father. He wasn't around during the times when she needed him the most. My question to her was, "Have you enlightened him about how you feel?" She responded saying, "No". This is when I proceeded to ask her probing questions. "Do you know why your father wasn't there?" "What type of relationship did your grandfather have with your father?" It was important for this young lady to understand the workings of generational curses. And the turns that take place in life that allocate unwanted decisions. Needless to say, we both learned during that one small time of discussion that her grandfather was not there for her father. Her father neglected her and never established a relationship with her as a result of that. Notice the pattern. Her father never learned the components of a father and daughter relationship, because his father was not there for him.

Sometimes it takes just a little willingness to understand the tricks used by the enemy to stimulate confusion. It is possible to understand and forgive those who have molested you, beat you, and cursed you out.......................... Even when Jesus was hanging on the cross after being humiliated and beaten, He expressed his love by saying, "Forgive them, for they know not what they do." How do you forgive that father that deserted you or that mother who molested you, then gave you up and left you on someone else's doorstep?

This is the time to fall on your knees and consult God. In turn, He will steer, direct, and give you the strength to overpower your circumstances. Seek God and give all of the control and responsibilities to God. His Spirit must be established, and then your desire to respond negatively becomes impossible.

Revenge!

The spirit of un-forgiveness shackles the mind and blinds the spiritual eyes, resulting in a hardened heart and a desire for revenge.

"Do not repay anyone evil for evil. Be careful to do what is right in the eyes of everybody.

If it is possible, as far as it depends on you, live at peace with everyone. Do not take revenge, my friends, but leave room for God's wrath, for it is written: "It is mine to avenge; I will repay," says the Lord. On the contrary; 'If your enemy is hungry, feed him; if he is thirsty, give him something to drink. In doing this, you will heap burning

coals on his head'. Do not be overcome by evil, but overcome evil with good.

Romans 12:17-21

You must grasp on to this concept and understand that there is no need to retaliate in your epoch of anger. God said, "It is mine to avenge; I will repay". Take some time out now and think of all the people who have mistreated you and you have not yet forgiven them. Write their names down on a sheet of paper. Then, make another list for those whom you have <u>fallen short with that need</u> to forgive you. If you think hard enough, your list may get pretty lengthy. Can you go to that person and say, "I was wrong and you don't deserve my anger?" Can you say to them, "I forgive you and I hope you will forgive me too?" It is now time to forgive and find a release from this fatal trap of guilt? The devil is a liar!

(Jesus speaking) For if you forgive men their trespasses, your heavenly father will also forgive you: But if you forgive not men their trespasses, neither will your father forgive your trespasses.

Matthew 6:14-15

It is a demonic spirit of un-forgiveness that causes brothers to kill brothers. That same demonic spirit deceivingly informs you to hate for impractical reasons. Revenge will not cause your hurts to diminish; it only confines your spirit into an imprisoned state.

In *Genesis 4:8*, the Bible talks about a man named Cain who failed to forgive his brother for a meaning without value. His inability to forgive and his great lack of self confidence, led him to murder his brother (by the way, this is the first recorded murder to ever take place).

Cain said to his brother Abel, "Let us go out to the field." And when they were in the field, Cain rose up against his brother Abel, and killed him. Then the Lord said to Cain, "Where is your brother Abel?" He said, I do not know; am I my brother's keeper?'

Genesis 4:8-9

Cain (firstborn), was the son of Adam and Eve. He was a farmer and his brother Abel (Second-born), was a shepherd. One day, they both brought offerings to God. Cain fetched grain from his crops and offered it to God. Abel, on the other hand, offered an animal from his flocks. Abel took time out and considered his offering. The Bible lets us know Abel brought to the Lord the finest he had. Cain, however, didn't put much thought at all into his offering. He just grabbed something from his field for the sake of not being empty handed. In contrast, Cain's offering is described as just an offering. The Bible lets us know that the Lord accepted Abel's offering and did not accept Cain's. This angered Cain. Cain convinced himself into believing that his offering was just as 0reciuos as Abel's. Cain felt that there was nothing wrong with his grain offering.

Your attitude determines your altitude

The offering in this case wasn't the problem; it was Cain's attitude that was. Cain's attitude was hideous. Cain's attitude toward God and toward others was faulty. Unlike his brother, Abel exuded an attitude of faith in God. Abel gave his offering to God with an undertone of the idea of love and compassion. Cain could have learned from his own mistakes and allowed God to speak to him, but instead he chose the sinners route.

"We must not be like Cain who was from the evil one and murdered his brother. And why did he murder him? Because his own deeds were evil and his brother's righteous."

I John 3:12

Cain allowed himself to be used and abused by the devil.

This is clear because he murdered his brother. He allowed the spirit of jealousy to overtake him. He knew Abel was a good and righteous man, and saw God's approval of Abel. Yet, he could not stand it. Cain was unable to admit his simple fault and forgive himself. Also, he wasn't successful at forgiving his brother, who did absolutely nothing wrong to him. Many times a simple conversation will solve the differences between two people. Instead, a conscious choice is made to bicker and many times this creates a fight. Cain should have talked to his brother and learned from his mistake. Abel understood the concept of sacrifice and Cain did not. Because Abel had the love of God in him, he could have explained to Cain that it was not the offering he brought, but the attitude in which he brought it. If Cain would have given Abel the chance to say, "Cain you gave the minimum of your heart and expected to receive a maximum reward from God, then Abel would not have died.

We do not know what was going on in Cain's mind; we all think differently. Most times we don't forgive because of misunderstanding or a lack of communication. We are a lot like Cain when we can't find it within ourselves to forgive others. We possess the same character when we become consumed with anger towards our brothers and sisters. Like Cain, our approach becomes entirely dominated by a self-centered, egotism. This is sin. We must overcome this sin and forgive with our hearts and not for the sake of formality.

"The LORD said to Cain, "Why are you angry, and why has your countenance fallen? If you do well, will you not be accepted? And if you do not do well, sin is lurking at the door; its desire is for you, but you must master it."

Genesis 4:6-7

God tried to work with Cain just as He tries daily to work with us. He wants us to become successful in conquering the battle of forgiveness, but we must be willing to receive from Him.

In effect, God said to Cain, "Abel made the best offering. Get over it! Don't be angry at Abel. Look at yourself. Change your attitude and do well and I will accept your offering." God's words were a challenge to Cain. Cain needed to get beyond the sin that was dominating your life.

Just as He was dealing with Cain, He deals with us. So you have gone through some mishaps in the past. Get over it! Love your enemies as you love yourself. Forgive and break free!

"Why do you look at the speck that is in your brother's eye, but do not notice the log that is in your own eye?"

Matthew 7:3

When they kept on questioning him, he straightened up and said to them, "If any one of you is without sin, let him be the first to throw a stone at her."

John 8:7

When God addresses you, He desires to be heard. If you are not in tune to hear His voice, you will miss your break through. Sometimes your own agenda hinders your ability to hear God. God tried to converse with Cain, but Cain was too engrossed in his anger. So, he paid no attention to God. Cain's own plan of sin back fired on him. Cain invited his brother to an open field and killed him. If you don't grab the idea of forgiving now, the enemy will dominate you, and you could possibly find yourself destined for hell. Your ultimate goal is to be free from hell.

Most mass and serial murderers don't possess the desire to forgive others. If they allowed Jesus into their hearts, they will find that He has the ability to soften their hearts, even if they are a vicious criminal. Many times we invite hurt and pain into our lives, because of our resistance to obey God. As Christians, we must learn to look for a reason to forgive. The person you need to forgive may be a mother, father, relative or friend. Prepare yourself mentally to forgive others just as God forgives you when you sin.

Being Judgmental Destroys Your Strength to Forgive

Many times, the judging of others faults stand in the way of your ability to forgive. Try not to look at the outer person without taking the time to see what really makes him/her who he/she is. For example, let's look at a cake. It may look good on the outside, but the inside is finished from a pile of sawdust glued together in a mode. We often see this type of wooden cake inside of a restaurant. They are called *sample cakes* and are designed to appear real and to desensitize your mind in hopes that you would spend money on a real cake that resemble the model. If you tried to cut this model cake, you will find that it is impossible to cut or eat. What I'm saying is, you cannot just look at the product, you must take a look inside and check out what it is made of. If you understand the heart of the person who has hurt you, it will become easier to pray and express mercy towards them. Prayer and mercy is better that resentment and unforgiving behavior. I firmly believe that if a person is changed on the inside, then it will show up on the outside.

The Bible introduces us to forms of judging. You can judge someone righteously with love in your heart, or you can judge someone unrighteously without love in your heart, resulting in your own opinion. Many times when unrighteous judging is practiced, slandering is entwined. The Bible tells us not to judge or we will be judged in the same manner. Be careful and not abuse this fine line!

Slander

> *Do not speak against one another, brethren. HE who <u>speaks against</u> a brother, or judges his brother, speaks against the law, and judges the law; but if you judge the law, you are not a doer of the law, but a judge of it.*

> *James 4:11*

The words, "speak against" in the scripture above, derives from the Greek word, "Katalaleo". It means to speak badly against someone and to dos so with an angered and unforgiving heart.

But you, why do you judge your brother? Or you again, why do you regard your brother with contempt? For we shall all stand before the judgment seat of God.

Romans 14:10

The people being spoken about in this passage of scripture were angry and refused to forgive others for what they were eating. The Apostle Paul was informing them that there was nothing wrong with eating or not eating (Romans 7:6-8). Their discrepancy was not about who was right or wrong, yet about being judgmental. So he says, "Do not judge one another".

Making Positive Judgments

There are four key times when we ought to be judgmental:

1. When we see another Christian committing sin.

"If your brother sins against you go and show him his fault, just between the two of you. IF he listens to you, you have won your brother over. But if he will not listen, take one or two others along, so that every matter may be established by the testimony of two or three witnesses. 'If he refuses to listen to them, tell it to the church; and if he refuses to listen even to the church, treat him as you would a pagan or a tax collector.

Matthew 18:15-17

Brothers, if someone is caught in a sin, you who are spiritual should restore him gently. But watch yourself, or you also may be tempted. *Galatians 6:1*

2. When we evaluate a person to be a leader in a church. They should be cautiously examined to fit many or all of the attributes illustrated in I Timothy, verse 3.

Here is a trustworthy saying: If anyone sets his heart on being an overseer, he desires a noble task. Now the overseer must be above reproach, the husband of but one wife, temperate, self-controlled, respectable, hospitable, able to teach, not given to drunkenness, not violent but gentle, not quarrelsome, not a lover of money. He must manage his own family well and see that his children obey him with proper respect. (If anyone does not know how to manage his own family, how can he take care of God's church?) He must not be a recent convert, or he may become conceited and fall under the same judgment as the devil. He must also have a good reputation with outsiders, so that he will not fall into disgrace and into the devil's trap. Deacons, likewise, are to be men worthy of respect, sincere, not indulging in much wine and not pursuing dishonest gain. They must keep hold of the deep truths of the faith with a clear conscience. They must first be tested; and then If there is nothing against them, let them serve as deacons.

I Timothy 3

Since an overseer is entrusted with God's work, he must be blameless not overbearing, not quick-tempered, not given to drunkenness, not violent, not pursuing dishonest gain. Rather he must be hospitable, one who loves what is good, who is self-controlled, upright, holy and disciplined. He must hold firm to the trustworthy message as it has been taught, so that he can encourage others by sound doctrine and refute those who oppose it.

Titus 1:7-9

3. Judge to decipher who the false/misleading teachers are.
4. We are expected to judge situations and determine whether or not the environment surrounding the situations is safe or pleasing to God for you to be occupied in.

Other than that, being judgmental toward others is not approved by God. Our duties are to be prayerful and to forgive them with a heart of love (Jesus).

Forgive Yourself

There is another aspect to forgiveness as well. Just like forgiving others, you must find it within yourself to forgive yourself. Don't get so caught up in the things of your past to where you become unable to continue in your future. The devil will allow your

77

past to become your new place of bondage. If you are still feeling sorry and crying over your past experience, then you have not forgiven yourself. I'm not saying that you should not repent for your wrong doings, but the Bible states:

> *If we confess our sins, he is faithful and just to forgive us of our sins, and cleanse us from all unrighteousness.*
>
> *I John 1:9*

Finding someone to teach about forgiving others come a dime a dozen. Rarely do we hear our leaders teaching about the importance of forgiving one's self. Forgiving you is much more difficult than forgiving others. Forgiving you is crucial to "breaking free". God doesn't desire for us to hold ourselves or others accountable, so much so, we become stuck and unmovable. Perhaps you have been successful at forgiving others, even for the most dreadful offenses. Yet you have failed to forgive yourself, for an equivalent or less serious offense. Perhaps you believe that forgiving yourself is not an option, because remembering your faults keep you in a place where you have always been: you'd rather stay in your comfort zone. Or maybe there are some things you have done that you are now convicted for, and you feel you have some form of lifelong atonement that you must pay for your past.

Forgiving yourself is not about forgetting. It is about remembering your past and becoming empowered by God and breaking free from your past. When God sees you, He only sees the, "now you". Once He has forgiven you, He only sees the "new you". Mark 2:5 says, "When Jesus saw their faith, he said to the paralytic, "Son, your sins are forgiven." God wants you to know that self forgiveness is easy and harmless.

Finally, brothers, whatever is true, whatever is noble, whatever is right, whatever is pure, whatever is lovely, whatever is admirable---if anything is excellent or praiseworthy---think about such things. Whatever you have learned or received or heard from me, or seen in me---put it into practice. And the God of peace will be with you.

Philippians 4:9

Forgiving yourself is appreciating you. Once you have forgiven you, no longer will the holding grudges on you be prevalent. You will no longer beat yourself up. Just as you would forgive an enemy for doing something wrong to you, you will forgive yourself. Once you have forgiven them, you become friends again. Freedom and laughter is now restored into the relationship. This is the same with you, once you have forgiven yourself that is when you, too, have become friends again with you. Forgiving yourself restores the joys of life back into you.

The person who has the ability to say, "I just can't forgive myself", is saying, "I am unwilling to take hold of and receive God's forgiveness." This type of people has put a harness around God and does not believe that God has forgiven them. Therefore, they are unable to forgive themselves. The guilt from inside has erased the idea of forgiving at all, from God and from themselves.

Top 5 Unforgiving Excuses. Which One Are You?

1. What I have done or where I have been wasn't that serious. We all have done something. There is no need for forgiving myself. **Try** – Become driven to seek God's grace and don't fool yourself by saying that your sin is not that bad. ALL SIN IS BAD!
2. It is God's will for me, no big deal. **Try** – Sin is a big deal. Sin causes Spiritual death. Don't underestimate God's hatred toward sin. You must release yourself from your sin. Forgive yourself.

"Woe to me!" I cried. "I am ruined! For I am a man of unclean lip, and I live among a people of unclean lips, and my eyes have seen the King, the LORD Almighty."

Isaiah 6:4

3. What I did was pretty bad. I don't think I could ever forgive myself, and I don't think I am worthy of God's forgiveness. **Try** – This person does not realize the depth of the desire God has to forgive His children. God forgives the worst of the worst sinners. He loves us all.

Do you know that the wicked will not inherit the kingdom of God? Do not be deceived: Neither the sexually immoral nor idolaters nor adulterers nor male prostitutes nor homosexual offenders nor thieves nor the greedy nor drunkards nor slanderers nor swindlers will inherit the kingdom of God. And that is what some of you were. But you were washed, you were sanctified, you were justified in the name of the Lord Jesus Christ and by the Spirit of our God.

I Corinthians 6:9-11

4. I just doubt God and this forgiving thing altogether. **Try** – This person is responding totally out of the will of God. Doubters are usually delayed by temptation. This includes Satan. He will lie to you and convince you to not believe what God has told you. Satan convinced Eve, but don't allow him to convince you!

Now the serpent was more crafty than any of the wild animals the LORD God had made. He said to the woman, "Did God really say, 'You must not eat from any tree in the garden'?"

Genesis 3:1

5. I ask for forgiveness, then, find myself sinning again. God does not have time for me anymore. **Try** – You repeat the sin over and over because you are experiencing what is called, "Growing up". Our spirit is maturing daily. Just keep trying and eventually you will prevail and God will continue to forgive.

Now that you have conquered forgiving you, it's now time to forgive others.

We are to put into practice those things that we have learned from God and from His Word. When you continue to rehearse in your thoughts the events of your transgression, then you are living against what Philippians 4:8 teaches us. The scripture instructs us to dwell on whatever is true, noble, right, pure, lovely, and admirable. Look for these attributes in yourselves. Move on!

How Do I Forgive Myself?

"...as far as the east is from the west, so far has he removed our transgressions from us."

Psalms 103:12

Psychiatric practices are partly responsible for popularizing the question. You may feel disappointed in yourself or you may be feeling as though you have failed to become successful, due to your past mistakes. Maybe you feel as though your habits are out of control, or life itself has become boring and has you discouraged. Whatever the reason for your negative feelings, you may need to examine your expectations, and re-determine whether or not you are just being too hard on yourself.

God has mercy on his credible creation. He loves you unconditionally, therefore, you need to love you. You can't love you and hold the past against you! You may become unrealistic to the expectations that you hold over your life. Two examples: Being disappointed with yourself because you stole from your parents when you were stuck in your drug addiction, or because you were the cause of your marriage going sour because you committed adultery.

> *You will again have compassion on us; you will tread our sins underfoot and hurl all our iniquities into the depths of the sea.*
>
> *Micah 7:19*

God has compassion on us and promises not to hold our past against us. We can only reach those things God allows us to reach and be who God wants us to be; nothing else!

Do you know that the devil will trick you into believing that you are less than the value in which God has created you? He is the number one self-esteem remover there is. The devil has spent his life time perfecting his plot to kill, steal, and destroy you. Killing, stealing, and destroying your self-esteem is enjoyable to him. He rips your self-esteem right from under your feet and gloats on your self dissatisfaction. The energy you use in harboring anger, hatred, and resentment towards yourself is a waste of time. If the Spirit of God is lacking in your spirit, your self-esteem is in danger. Every bit of energy you give in dwelling on your past regrets now robs you of the energy you need to become the person who God created you to become. Satan does not want you to know that you are fearfully and wonderfully made by God. As long as the enemy can continue to convince you that you are less than who God had made you to be, he can control you. This is why it is very important that you understand the importance of forgiving yourself. Forgiving yourself is a conscious choice that takes courage and strength to do, and it gives you the opportunity to become an overcomer, rather than remaining a victim of your own scorn.

When you can find it within yourself to forgive others and not yourself, you are sending a subliminal message to yourself saying, "I am less capable of making a poor decision than others". What does this mean? You are now saying, "I am perfect and without excuses, therefore, I should not forgive myself when I fall." When this happens, you have now stepped into the shoes of Jesus. Jesus' job is His and you are powerless in attempting to operate with yourself pride in His shoes.

"Pride goes before destruction and a haughty spirit before a fall."

Proverbs 16:18

Not forgiving yourself will invite self-destruction, a haughty spirit, and a hard downfall. Once you learn and take heed to the idea that self forgiveness brings upon peace, you will then begin to experience a life of tranquility, worship, and delight.

When milk spills and runs off the table, your wisdom informs your mind that the milk is now polluted and is not healthy to drink. It will be just unsafe to soak it up with an absorber of some sort, and then wring the milk back into the glass.

Face it, the milk has become undrinkable and must be cleaned up and discarded. Once it spills, it's gone. We can't go back and change what has already been done. We can't erase the hurt feelings of those we have hurt in the past, but we can make a difference by cleaning it up and discarding the hurt. A great way to begin is to first forgive yourself and then others. Forgive yourself and let the healing begin! I invite you to break the chains that have you bound.

Forgiving yourself is a great road to travel towards freedom of the chains that keep us in bondage. Pray freely to Jesus and let Him know what has kept you angry, as it pertains to your own mistakes, and regrets. Stay in your Bible! You will be surprised at how the Lord sends you right to the perfect scriptures that will relate to your circumstances. That's what makes the Bible so unique. Every scripture promotes healing to every one in need. Don't blame God for your trauma; use Him for your deliverance. Invite Jesus into your tender spots, and realize this. He is the ultimate answer to your problem. Jesus knows the way to restoring hope and purpose back into your life.

Life is too short to spend excessive time being angry about your bad times. Being angry with someone for what they have done to you in the past is also a waste of your precious life time. Self-anger and disappointments poison your spirit. Being angry is being out of control. It's time to break free! Just make up your mind today that this is the right thing to do, and that on today no one will stop you. Make a decision not to allow anyone who has done wrong to you to control your destiny. What if God decided to act like you and hold grudges toward you? Think about all of the times He has forgiven you and others you know and love. At least show your gratitude to Him by obeying His command to forgive others and yourself. Always be willing to forgive, even when people have despitefully and deliberately wronged you or even if you have wronged yourself and God. Forgiveness doesn't depend on what you consider fair, reasonable, or just. It's a matter of being faithful to God. Don't wait until you feel like forgiving someone; you probably never will. Instead, make a heartfelt and sincere decision to do so, and trust God to help you that very moment. Tomorrow, or five minutes from now is not promised. Expect God to clear bitterness out of your heart, then step out and begin forgiving.

Say this prayer if you would like to be set free.

Heavenly Father,

I thank you for giving me the knowledge to know that I, too, can be forgiven. Not only by you, but also I can forgive myself, for myself, and by myself. Lord, remove me from my place of not being friends with myself. As I release my past, now, and future to you, I am asking that you will never allow me to revisit my present state again. I want to continue further seeking you. I realize now Jesus that I don't have time to focus on what can't save me anymore. I want to break free, in Jesus name.

Chapter Four

Don't Go Back

***Stand fast in the liberty wherewith Christ hath made us free,
and be not entangled again with the yoke of bondage.***

Galatians 5:1

It is important that once God has freed you from the things
that had you bound, that you do not revert back to repeat those same
scenarios again. One of the simplest ways to have a relapse of an
addiction is to go back to doing the same things. Going back to your
place of vulnerability is not wise. Lot's wife turned into a pillar of
salt when she looked back on the city of Sodom where she had been
delivered from. When you have been delivered, reverting back to the
place where you have been freed from can be tragic. Many times
people have been delivered from abusive relationships only to return
back to relive the same tragic life. If your abuser has not sought and
accepted Jesus Christ as their savior, more than likely, you returning
back to his intended safe arms, would not be wise. Statistics have
proven the abuse would most likely continue. Your abusers cannot
change themselves, only God can!

Your life is not controlled by those things that are out of the
will of God. It is vitally important that once the shackles and
strongholds have been broken that you don't revert back.

You must not hang around and mingle with the problem.

But, I Love My Spouse.

In relationships we try so hard at times to make them work even though the spouse is abusive. "But, I love my spouse; He is the parent of my child." We must realize that we cannot change the heart of an abuser; we can only leave and give them over to God. God is the only real mind regulator. Considering, returning can be a dangerous situation. Once your mind begins to agree that you will go back, you will become stuck again. It is safer to hear from God, who is the controller of your mind and thoughts. If the thought of returning becomes overwhelming, fall down on your knees in submission, and begin to plead the Blood of Jesus. Only He can give you the strength you need to "break free" from those binding chains. Continue to press on, for your strength is on the way. The more you press forward, the stronger you will become. If you want to gain this strength you must have the Lord on your side.

"And behold, there came a man named Jairus, and he was a ruler of the synagogue: and he fell down at Jesus' feet, and besought him that he would come into his house: For he had only one daughter, about twelve years of age, and she lay a dying. But as he went the people thronged him. And a woman having an issue of blood twelve years, which had spent all her living upon physicians, neither could be healed of any, came behind him, and touched the border of his garment: an immediately her issue of blood stanched. And Jesus said, who touched me? When all denied, Peter and they that were with him said, Master, the multitude throng thee and press thee, and sayest thou, Who touched me? And Jesus said, Somebody hath touched me: for I perceive that virtue is gone out of me. And when the woman saw that she was not hid, she came trembling, and falling down before him, she declared unto him before all the people for what cause she had touched him, and how she was healed immediately. And he said unto her, Daughter, be of good comfort; thy faith had made thee whole; go in peace.

Luke 8:41-48

Be like the woman with the issue of blood. The Bible tells us, this woman was in the midst of a crowd, trying desperately to get to Jesus. I imagine many were pushing and shoving, because they too wanted to see or touch Jesus. She could have given up, threw in the towel, and turned back, but she didn't. She was persistent and continued to press forward, believing Jesus to be her healer. She knew that if she could only get to Jesus, her problems would be solved. So, she remained steadfast until she got to Jesus. You must do the same. Keep pressing on no matter how strong the temptation gets! Fight your way through the crowd and make your way to Jesus. The journey won't be easy, because the enemy is going to try to block your way, but through your prayers and persistence, you can make it to Jesus, and He will feel your touch and set you free.

The joy of the Lord is your strength.

Nehemiah 8:10

The Bible gives many solutions as to why we should and can continue to press forward and not turn back to our past. If we stay in constant fellowship with fellow believers, statistics have shown and proven that the odds for returning back are slim. When you are in constant fellowship with others who love the Lord, you all now have the ability to agree with one another in prayer regarding your circumstances. Now you are in fellowship in an environment surrounded by God and all of His provisions. Studies have proven that an alcoholic or drug addict would never relapse if they remained in fellowship with a higher power (Jesus). Those who were in an abusive relationship will hardly ever return back to them if they are involved in a positive fellowship and rely on a high power (Jesus).

If you want to be free from your past, it would be wise to find a constant and loving church where you can go and fellowship with those who are filled with the Spirit of God. Look for a church that has a firm Bible teaching leader and who is not ashamed to teach, speak, and live the truth. You want a fellowship that is organized and driven by Jesus Christ. Look for a church that teaches only what the Word of God says. If Jesus is not in the forefront, it would not be wise for you to fellowship there. There is only one God-lead fellowship that has lasted nearly two-thousand years and has provided millions of souls to total freedom and deliverance. Including Jesus is the only guaranteed way of not returning. Remember this, Jesus is in charge.

We proclaim to you what we have seen and heard, so that you also may have fellowship with us. And our fellowship is with the Father and with his Son, Jesus Christ. We write this to make our joy complete.

I John 1:3

Bondage Loose Me In The Name of Jesus!

God doesn't expect His people to be in bondage! Read your Bible! It's there! God has delivered you from the bondage of sin, drugs, alcohol, fear, doubt, the devil, false ideas, immorality, bitterness, an unforgiving spirit, iniquity, greed, selfishness, pride, jealousy, lust money and whatever else the devil uses to control and drive your life.

"If the son therefore shall make you free, ye shall be free indeed."

John 8:36

Then he saith, I will return into my house from whence I came out; and when he is come, he findeth it empty, swept, and garnished. Then goeth he, and taketh with himself seven other spirits more wicked than himself, and they enter in and dwell there: and the last state of that man is worse than the first. Even so shall it be also unto this wicked generation.

Matthew 12:44-45

My husband shared a story with me concerning a time in his life when he was young and unstable. He said the elderly people loved him so much, because they thought he was such a good child, because of how he behaved while in their presence. He went on to tell me about the time he had received and accepted his calling into the ministry. He did not accept his calling immediately. He wanted to escape the entire idea of it and would have been pleased with himself by just making a conscious decision to live right. In making that decision, he stopped committing all of his secret sins that were only seen by God and he went to church every Sunday. Needless to say, this only lasted a short time. He reverted back to doing the things he used to do but, this time his sins were seven times worse than they were before. He was a mess! At this point my husband did not care about who saw him in sin. He transformed from a bold man of God to a bold sinner of Satan's. This is because the level and intensity of the demonic forces against him had increased. Why? During the time my husband spent with the Lord, the ways and notions of God were being deposited into his spirit. Therefore the enemy now needed his stronger forces to attempt to confuse and suppress the newly deposited knowledge of God, in which my husband was receiving. This is why the sins were now intensified. This is what happens when you decide to go back.

While ministering at the women's shelter, I see so many, women that has come from abusive relationships, or battling drug addictions, and is progressing spiritually by leaps and bounds. They are in high spirits, their countenance has improved, but then without warning, they make the mistake of going back to the same environment that originally caused their pain. Some of them return back to the shelter in a far worse condition than they were in the beginning. Whatever you do, don't go back! Stand fast in the liberty, wherewith Christ has made you free.

Chapter Five

Rejoice

And all the people saw him walking and praising God.

Acts 3:9

When you have received the salvation of the Lord, and have confessed that you have matters that only God can handle, you are now equipped to give God praise. When you have learned how to forgive yourself and those who have hurt or harmed you and have chosen not to go back, you have now stepped into the arena to begin worship to God. When the Spirit of God has merged with your spirit, you can't help but to **rejoice!**

We all have reasons to rejoice after conquering difficult situations and breaking free from addictions and abuse that had us bound. I, myself, leap for joy whenever I feel shackles being loosed from me; when I am loosed from the bondages that had entered my life. Experiencing the feeling of the chains being broken is inexpressible, especially knowing that it was God that loosed me.

Let's take a look at what was happening when Peter said to the man in Acts:

In the name of Jesus Christ of Nazareth, rise up and walk. And he took him by his right hand, and lifted him up; and immediately his feet and ankle bones received strength. And he leaping up stood, and walked and entered with them into the temple, walking and leaping, and praising God.

Acts 3:6b-8

The man in the scripture above was excited because he was now free from his lifelong illness that had him bound. Praise the Lord!

He was lame from his mother's womb. But now, The Lord has freed him from his bondage and he is rejoicing.

Acts 3:2

It is no wonder this man was rejoicing. He had every reason to celebrate. He had never walked a day in his life, now suddenly, thanks to Jesus Christ, he could walk and leap. Just that alone was the generator of his rejoicing and yes, we are born sinners, placed in bondage, and have no control over the state in which God allows us to be born in. But, we do have a choice of whether we would like to remain in that state or come out. You may have been born to a crack-addict mother, to abusive parents, or into a family where there is a demon of sexual molestation is raging fierce. However, you should know that your life does not end there; it is just beginning.

The man in the story was born unable to walk, but God changed his situation and delivered him from that bondage. God wishes to do the same thing for you. I want you to know that you don't have to stay under the shadow of the circumstances in which you were born into. It really doesn't matter how or where you were born, your situation is destined for greatness. You can get out; you can be freed by the power of the almighty God. God finds great pleasure in you rejoicing in Him with admiration for him. Even God enjoys feeling appreciated.

Serve the Lord with gladness; come before his presence with singing. Be thankful unto him and bless his holy name.

Psalms 100:2

Praise him for his mighty acts; when God has performed the mighty act of setting us free from things that had us bound it is time to rejoice!

Psalms 150:2a

And all the people saw him walking and praising God.

Acts 3:9

I will bless the LORD at all times: his rejoicing shall continually be in my mouth. My soul shall make her boast in the LORD: the humble shall hear thereof, and be glad.

O magnify the Lord with me, and let us exalt his name together. I sought the LORD, and he heard me, and delivered me from all my fears. They looked unto him, and were lightened: and their faces were not ashamed. This poor man cried, and the LORD heard him, and saved him out of all his troubles. The angel of the LORD encamped round about them that fear him, and delivered them. O taste and see that the Lord is good: blessed is the man that trusted in him.

Psalms 34:1-8

Rejoicing in the Lord is important because Jesus enjoys the praise. It's very important to realize how much rejoicing should be a part of our lifestyles. Rejoicing in the Lord is a part of you that will become uncontrollable. Once the old man in you becomes the new creature in God, rejoicing instantly becomes a part of you. When you rejoice, you are expressing an act of approval or admiration for the many things Jesus has done. Rejoicing can be expressed in a variety of ways. Rejoicing can be expressed by way of a song, poem, dance, or words that convey enormous positive reception. Other times rejoicing is expressed through praise and worship. Praise shows admiration to the work of God, and worship shows the admiration for what God has done. Rejoicing is important because it assures the Lord as to where we are and how we feel towards Him. Our hearts should always be centered on the Lord. You should always find time to stop and rejoice in the Lord, not only because it pleases Him, but because He again, has kept you in His loving arms of protection. David informs us that we should give the Lord His due time. If you rejoice in God, He will find delight in you.

Our obedience encourages God to do as He promised. As long as we continue to rejoice and be obedient to Him, He will continue to do what He promised us.

Get out of the habit of rejoicing in the Lord only because you have received and answered prayer. Learn to rejoice in the Lord because of who He is. Even when times seem at their worse than they have ever been, rejoice in God for the victory that will come in the end. Often, this is where we tend to miss it. The Bible says, **"Faith is the substance of things hoped for, and the evidence of**

things not seen." In knowing this, you should rejoice in God for the things that will come to pass.

There's time for us to get our rejoicing on individually and there's time for corporate rejoicing. In other words, we can rejoice in the Lord all alone or in a congregation of other saints. Whichever way it comes, rejoicing is essential to your Christian walk! We were created to give glory to the Lord 'through our lives.' One tragic mistake man often make is when he fails to obey the Psalms 100 that says:

> **Make a joyful noise unto the LORD, all ye lands. Serve the LORD with gladness: come before his presence with singing. Know ye that the LORD he is God: it is he that hath made us, and not we ourselves; we are his people, and the sheep of his pasture, Enter into his gates with thanksgiving, and into his courts with praise: be thankful unto him and bless his name. For the LORD is good; his mercy is everlasting; and his truth endureth to all generations.**

We need to give glory to God by rejoicing, for He deserves it, and we are nothing without Him.

I can do all things through Christ which strengtheneth me.

Philippians 4:13

We can't make it without the Lord. Face it! Life has no real meaning without Him. We exist, but that's about it. There is a cliché': "God is good all the time and all the time God is good." Well, if you live for Him, you'll attest that this statement is indeed true without a shadow of a doubt. There is nothing like experiencing the Lord for yourself. There is none like Him (Jesus). It doesn't matter how many times someone shares their testimony with you, it will never mean as much until you have experienced the move of God yourself. Taste and see how good God is! I dare you to! He is indeed good! Try Him today, for tomorrow may be too late. Tomorrow is not promised to any of us. Give your life to Him totally, and without any regrets. Jesus gave His life, was resurrected, ascended into heaven, and is coming back again. God is good whether you rejoice in Him or not. Trust me as I tell you this. The more you rejoice, the sooner you'll begin to see Him move like never before in your life. We have so much to be thankful for! It is my prayer that you be blessed, be encouraged, be prayerful, and constantly rejoicing in Him. May God bless you as you BREAK FREE!

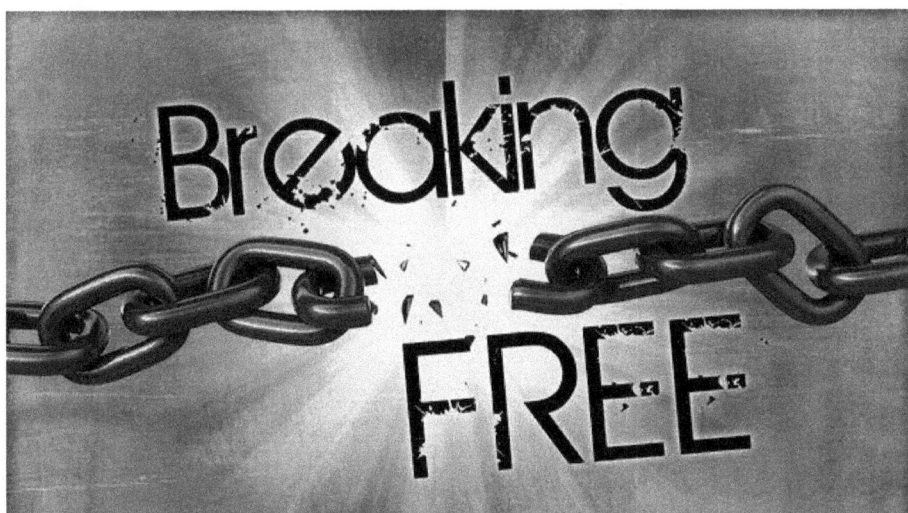

CLOSING THOUGHTS

When I begin to look at the steps that were ordered by God, I know that He walked me through these chapters. Salvation is the first step to new life. The Word plainly speaks, "Seek ye first the Kingdom of God and all these things shall be added." So that particular word alone is the path to take, open your heart and receive Jesus. Bondage will not remain if you allow God to operate in your broken state. Allow Him to be the center of your life and everything else will subject itself.

www.ingramcontent.com/pod-product-compliance
Lightning Source LLC
Chambersburg PA
CBHW062007040426
42447CB00010B/1951